**This book is to be returned on or before
the last date stamped below.**

Castles

Castles

Henry Pluckrose

Mills & Boon ON LOCATION Book no. 4

Photographs by Alec Davis
Drawings by Chris Evans

(opposite)
Round tower on the curtain wall of
Beaumaris Castle, Anglesey, one of the
many castles built by Edward I in the
thirteenth century

MILLS & BOON Limited, London

First published in Great Britain 1973
by Mills & Boon Limited, 17–19
Foley Street, London W1A 1DR.

ISBN 0 263 05307 5 (cased)
ISBN 0 263 05426 8 (limp)

Printed in Great Britain by
W & J Mackay Limited, Chatham
Bound by Hunter & Foulis,
Edinburgh

Contents

Chepstow Castle gatehouse built of rough limestone rubble, 1225–45. The Guard Room Tower is on the left and the Prison Tower on the right

Preface

This is not just another book on castles – it is rather a book of clues to help you look more closely at the castles you visit.

It is written for the young person who wants to know what to look for in and around a castle and how to record the things he sees.

But I hope it will be of use to older people too who, like me, wander round the castles that dot the countryside and wonder at their size and the sophistication of their defences.

July 1972   *H.P.*

1 Why castles?

I wonder if you have ever paused to think about the buildings you pass as you travel by car, coach or bike along an English road? Some of the buildings, atomic power stations for example, are very new; others, like churches, quite old. Each building, if we look at it carefully, will tell us something about the people for whom it was built. We could begin by examining the material that has been used (wood, stone, concrete, steel, glass) and the way it has been worked. Then we might ask why the building was put up at all, what it was for, what things the architect had to bear in mind when deciding upon a particular plan or design.

Now that might sound very complicated. But think for a moment of a modern house. What would your parents require? They would need some sleeping space (bedrooms), spaces for cooking, washing and daytime living. The building would need at least one entrance and some openings (windows) for letting in the daylight. It should keep out the

Norman carved tympanum on doorway leading to the ground floor of the Great Tower at Chepstow Castle

worst of the weather and have some form of internal heating. Now these requirements are almost the same as those of your great-grandparents who were young when Queen Victoria was on the throne. Nowadays, of course, the builder would provide central heating rather than open fires, electric points in the kitchen rather than a coal oven, a garage rather than a stable. He has slightly altered his plan to meet the requirements of his time, but his purpose remains much the same . . . to provide a place in which a family can live in reasonable comfort (and what is reasonable comfort now would have been the height of luxury a hundred years ago).

But what, you might say, has any of this to do with castles? Put simply, I would like you to begin by thinking of castles as buildings which were made to meet a particular need and which changed (just as our houses have) in the light of new discoveries and inventions. Their purpose remained the same across the centuries (a stronghold) and as soon as they could no longer perform it, their importance declined and they were no longer built.

However, before we begin to look at
the castle we really need to under-
stand how it developed from a simple
wooden tower on a mound of earth
to the massive fortifications at
Berkeley, Warwick or Beaumaris.
Why, when over a period of 500
years military architects had per-
fected the castle as a secure stronghold, did its value decline so rapidly?

By visiting castles and by finding the
clues (which are still there for us to
see) you will not only learn how to
look but go some way to answering
the questions with which I wanted
to begin this book. 'Why *did* people
build castles, why did they stop – and
why don't we build castles today?'

2 How castles developed

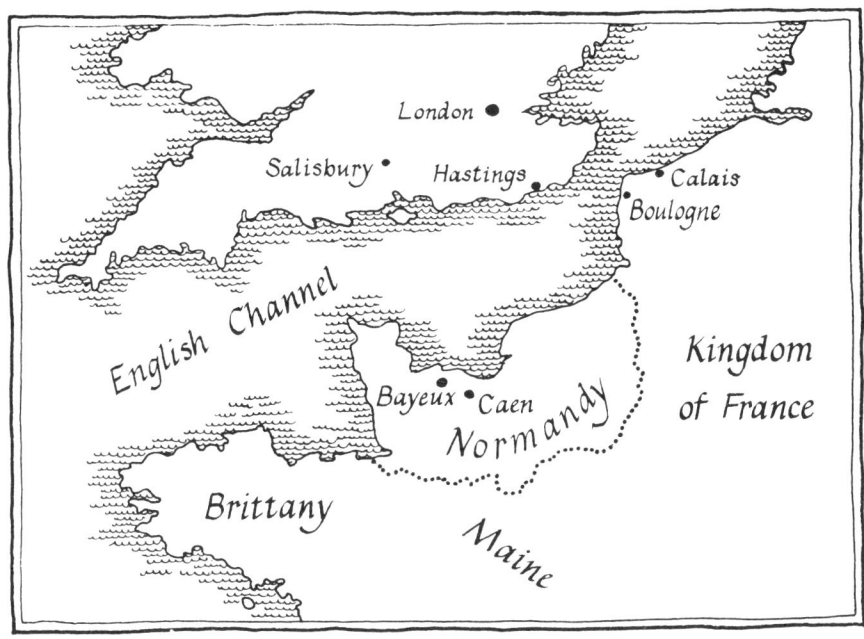

England and Normandy at the time of the Battle of Hastings

Undoubtedly, the best-known date in English history is 1066. This was the year in which William, Duke of Normandy, came across the channel with his army and defeated Harold Godwinson at the Battle of Hastings.

Most history books tell of the events which preceded the battle – of how Harold was shipwrecked off the coast of Normandy and, taken before Duke William, swore an oath that when

King Edward the Confessor died, he would support William's claim to the crown of England. Harold argued that he only gave this promise to obtain his freedom and that an oath given under threat meant nothing.

William, we know, was extremely angry when he heard that Harold had not kept his promise and

immediately began to prepare to
invade England. He gathered a fleet
to carry his army across the channel.
His army consisted of heavily-
armoured knights, archers and foot
soldiers. In addition to the fighting
men, space had to be found in the
boats for war horses and numerous
craftsmen (like armourers, smiths and
carpenters) on whom the soldiers
depended.

*A drawing from the Bayeux Tapestry
showing workmen building the motte of
Hastings Castle*

But Duke William was an experienced soldier. He had lived through
many campaigns in France and knew
that he must make space on his war
fleet for a 'castle'. Now it's obvious
that William couldn't hope to take
a great stone tower on his small
wooden ships. But he could do the
next best thing. This was to have his
carpenters shape and trim wood
from the forests of Normandy, cutting
joints and boring peg holes in the
pieces so that a wooden castle could
be erected as soon as the army
landed in England. The Bayeux
Tapestry – which tells the story of

the events leading up to the Conquest – shows barrels being carried aboard. Some are obviously wine, but others are among the military stores, and there is some reason to think that they may have held pegs to fix the timber framework. William's advisers seem to have thought of everything!

This wooden castle was certainly not the first castle to be built in England. The Romans and the Celts before them had built forts and castles which gave protection in time of trouble. Indeed it is probable that in the reign of Edward the Confessor an attempt had been made to improve the defences at Dover (which had been a stronghold since Roman times). We also know that Edward had employed a Norman knight to build a castle in Shropshire.

Thus, although castles were not unknown in England before William's victory, they became quite commonplace in the years that followed upon it. The defeat of Harold at Hastings had made William king – but he still had to prevent the English from rising against his rule. One way of doing this was for William to erect strongholds across the country, placing each stronghold under the command of a knight on whose loyalty he could rely. These strongholds could serve many purposes – barracks for soldiers, a place from which armed patrols could be sent through the neighbouring country-side, a fortress to retreat to if there was an uprising. The constable of the castle (the knight holding it for the king) could also use it as a court where the king's laws were enforced, a prison for criminals and law-breakers and a centre for the collection of local taxes.

So the castle had to be a place:

1 Which could be defended against attack.

2 Which was large enough to house a large number of people (soldiers, household servants, skilled craftsmen, lawyers and priests as well as the lord's family and the families of his 'chief retainers' (or captains).

3 Which could be self-supporting for a period of time. Water and food had to be available in time of siege. Thus many castles had a large courtyard in which live animals could be kept until they were required in the kitchen. Similarly all castles were built over a supply of water. Usually a well was dug, for this meant that the water could not be poisoned or cut off by enemies, outside the castle walls.

The first castles that the Normans built were little more than wooden forts (though two of our most famous stone castles – at London and at Colchester – were begun by William). The interesting thing is that these early castles followed a similar

*The very first castles were little more than
wooden forts consisting of motte,
palisade and wooden tower*

pattern. At first a circular mound of earth – **a motte** – was thrown up. Much of the earth for the mound was dug from around its base. Thus a ditch was formed which, when filled with water, became the **moat.** The mound was flattened on top and on this a wooden fence was built. This was called the **palisade.** Inside the palisade a wooden house was built for the lord and his retainers.

The castle was often extended by adding a **bailey.** This was a large courtyard beyond the motte. It was also banked and palisaded and its ditch ran into the ditch running round the motte.

The bailey provided space for storage, stables, workshops and a chapel. It was also an outer defence for the lord's stronghold.

Imagine for a moment that you wanted to visit the Lord who lived in the castle shown here. You would have to cross the narrow footbridge, pass the guard, cross the bailey, go over the second bridge, through another defended gate and then into the tower or 'donjon' itself. Usually the ground floor of the tower was only storage space. To reach the Lord's hall you would have to climb a ladder to the doorway on the first floor.

The simple hill fort grows larger with the addition of a bailey

Now imagine that you are an enemy attacking the castle. All the entrances are defended, the palisades are manned with archers and the bridges and ladders have been removed or destroyed. Although the motte and bailey castle seems a simple place to capture, it could hold out against a much greater force. The defenders were always able to shoot down on their attackers – and they even took precautions against fire bombs by hanging animal skins soaked in water along the palisades and over the roofs of the buildings.

During William's reign (1066–1087), over one hundred large motte and bailey castles were built and many of these earthworks are visible today. When visiting a castle which can be traced back to Norman times, look for the outline motte and bailey. Does the shape remind you of a number 8? Sometimes you will find interesting variations. At Lewes, for example, there are two mottes joining one bailey so we have a chain shape. At Lincoln there are two mottes inside one bailey.

As time went by some of these motte and bailey castles fell into disrepair and disuse. Others were developed, the wooden walls and towers being replaced by stronger ones of stone. It's worth remembering that the Normans were very skilled builders and it would have been very unwise to have built a stone tower on top of a hurriedly thrown-up pile of loose earth. The earth had to be allowed to settle before tons of stonework could be placed upon it. Not that castles were always built on man-made mottes. Where possible natural hills were used, particularly if a small river ran near by to provide an extra line of defence, or a natural moat.

Many of the stone towers which were built during the reigns of the kings who followed **William the Conqueror** (William II, Henry I, Stephen, Henry II) can still be seen today, and though many of them are very ruined, it is easy to imagine how impressive they must have been when alive with the sounds of people and animals.

Motte and bailey castles – three variations in plan

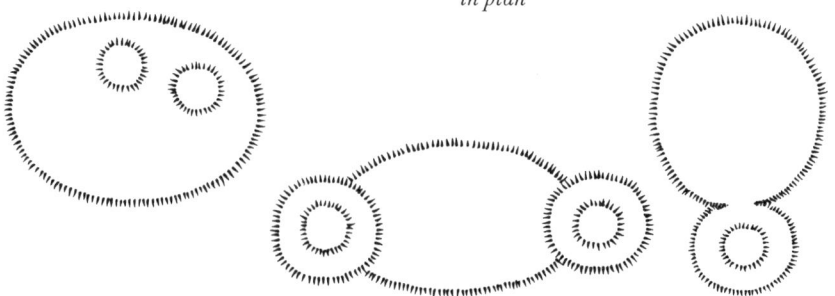

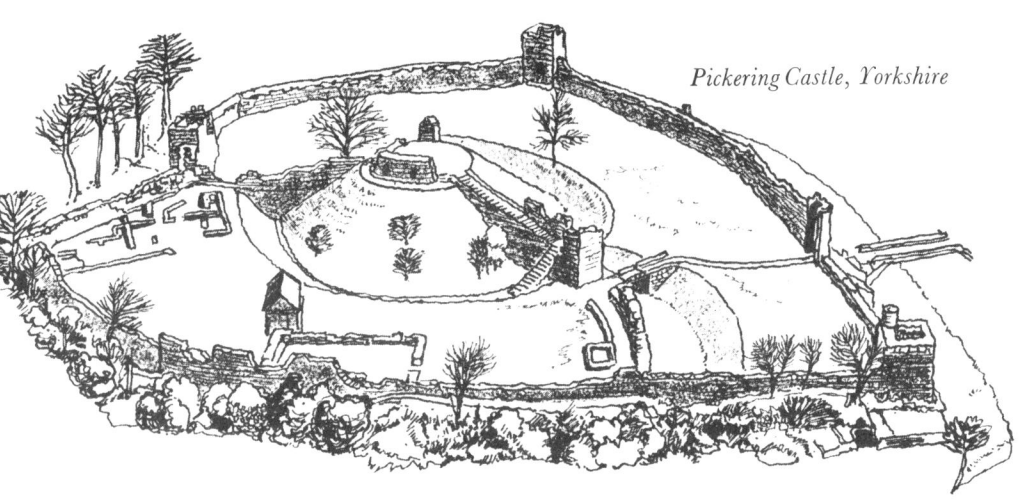

Pickering Castle, Yorkshire

Sometimes a natural hill was used for a castle

The development of Norwich Castle

To make the keep even more difficult
to capture, the walls around it were
also built of stone. This stone wall
was known as a **curtain.** It enclosed
a courtyard (or ward) similar to the
bailey of the early castles. Similarly
the gatehouse which protected the
drawbridge, was also made of stone.

At about the same time as this, other
architects were experimenting with
another design. A circular stone wall
was built around the top of the motte.
This formed a stone shell which we

*Shell keep at Restormel Castle,
Cornwall . . .*

. . . and at Launceston Castle, Cornwall

call a **shell keep.** The various buildings which we would expect to find
in a castle nestle against this external
wall leaving a courtyard in the centre.

*Square Norman keep, about 100 feet
high, Rochester Castle, Kent*

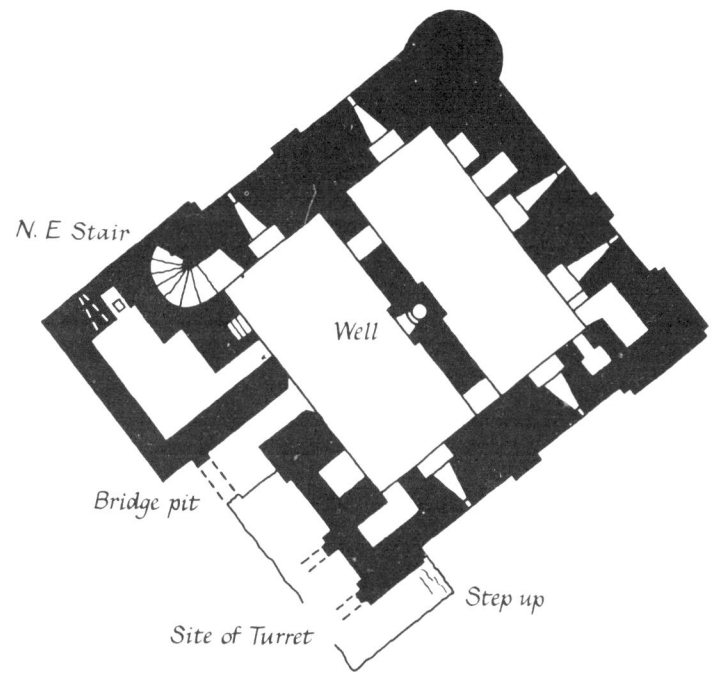

Ground floor plan of Rochester Castle

There are famous shell keeps at Windsor, Arundel and Restormel (Cornwall).

But the great square keeps did not answer all the problems of warfare. To begin with the corners were weak and if successfully mined (see page 89) or battered with a ram, great damage could be done to the building. Then the defenders found it hard to see all the attackers without leaning over the walls. If the walls were curved or rounded, would defence be easier?

At Orford Castle (Suffolk) the keep was built on a polygonal plan. Each turret supported its neighbour and every inch of the ground below could be overlooked from above. The round keep had two other advantages. It used less stone and was easier to roof.

Keeps of this type also allowed the castle dwellers to live more comfortably. The turrets provided defence and extra living space.

Square Norman keep faced with ashlar, Goodrich Castle, Herefordshire. The first-floor entrance has been converted to a trefoiled window (opposite)

Circular Norman keep, Conisbrough Castle, Yorkshire

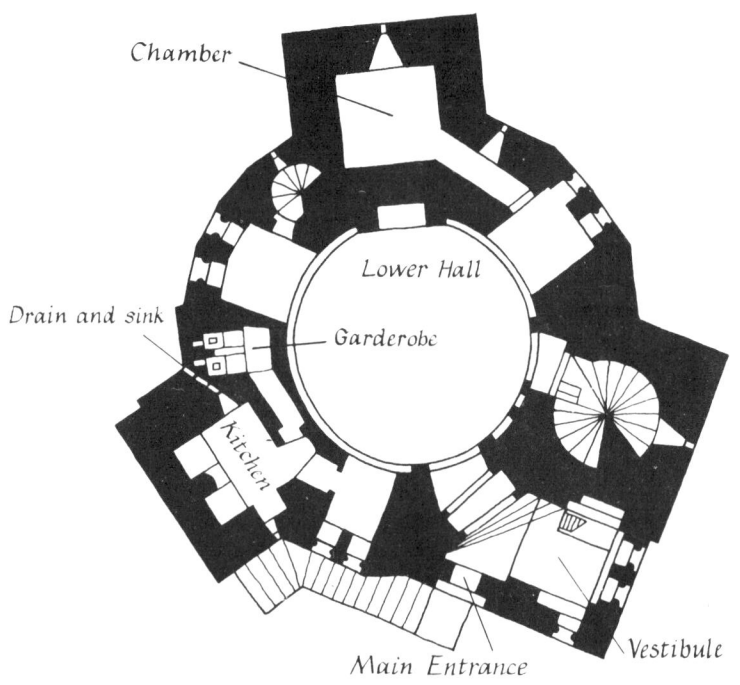

Ground floor plan of Orford Castle

But it was found that the great keep with its curtain walls was not secure against a determined enemy. If the curtain wall was captured then all the important stores were captured too. Towers were therefore erected along the length of the wall to give additional protection. These towers (sometimes called mural towers) often jutted out from the wall so that they overlooked the ground immediately beneath the walls – which meant that attackers would find it difficult to mine or use battering rams. A rain of arrows from two towers could make it impossible for the enemy to dig the mine tunnel or bring up siege equipment (see Chapter 7).

Experience gained from the round keeps encouraged the castle builders to give no corners to the towers along the curtain walls. We know that round or D-shaped towers were stronger and cheaper in materials. Another advantage was that enemy missiles tended to bounce off a curved wall without doing too much damage.

Round Norman keep, Orford Castle, Suffolk

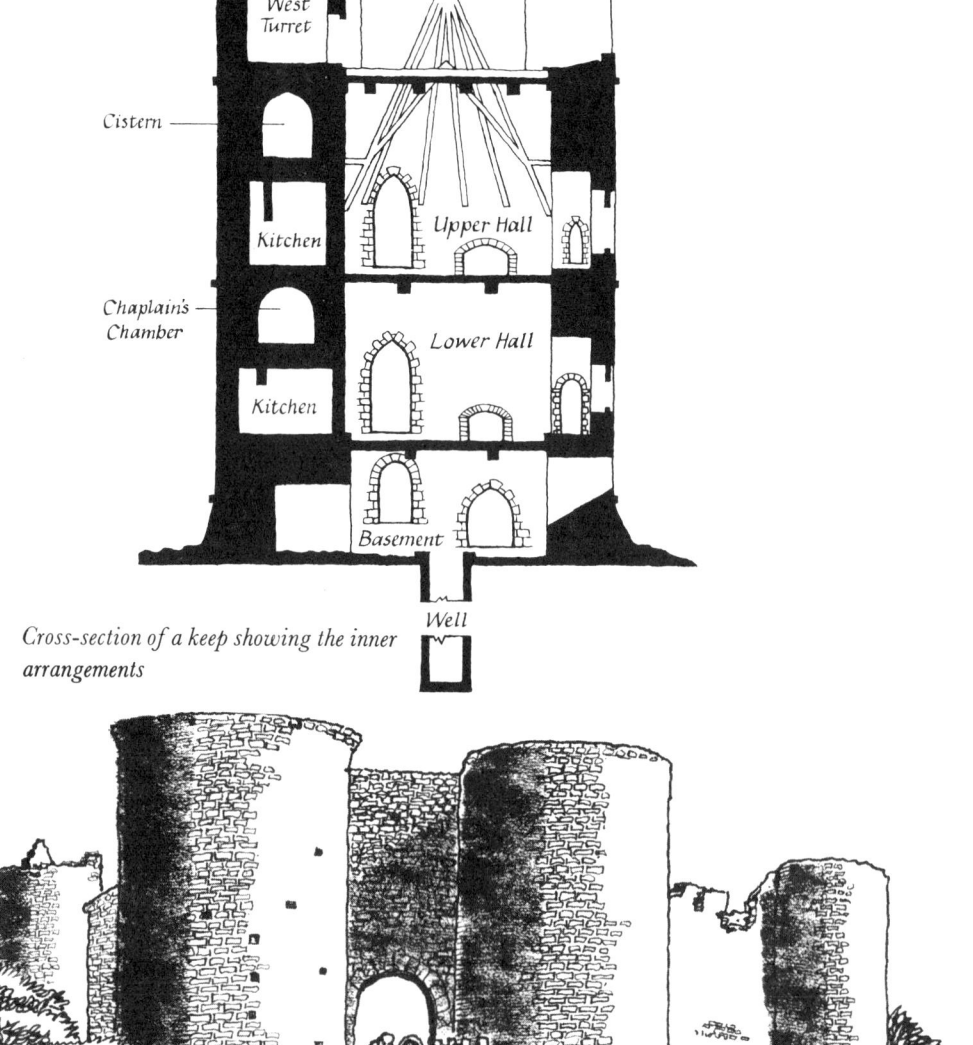

Cross-section of a keep showing the inner arrangements

Mural towers on the curtain wall of White Castle, Monmouth

The towers were built so that they were taller than the curtain walls which lay between them. This meant that if part of the wall were stormed, defenders could still fire down arrows on the attackers from the towers. The capturing of part of the wall did not mean that the whole of the bailey (and the stores it contained) was in danger.

More mural towers, Conway Castle, Caernarvonshire, but this time with well-preserved battlements

So more ground began to be taken up by the castle's defences. Look at this drawing of Dover Castle. It is based on an old print. In the centre is the great keep built by Henry II in stone in the 1180s. During the years that followed, more and more energy was spent on extending the outer defences to make it even more difficult to capture. More walls and towers meant that more ground was used and the castle grew outwards from the central point of its strength, the keep or **donjon.** We get the word dungeon (a place for keeping prisoners) from the word **donjon**

(which means a safe place to be – thus it was a place from which prisoners would find it difficult to escape, a place where they would be held safely).

As the walls became more difficult to storm, it became obvious (if you wanted to capture a castle) that the best way into the bailey was through the gatehouse . . . and if the gatehouse were made so strong that there was little chance of it being captured, was there any need for a keep inside the walls at all?

Dover Castle

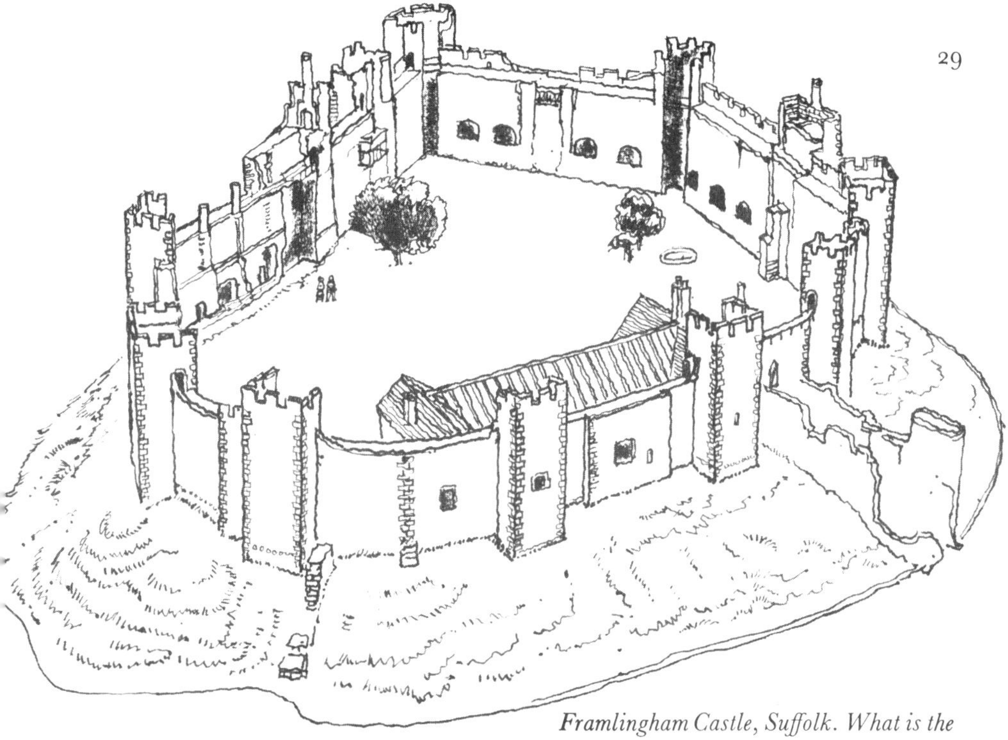

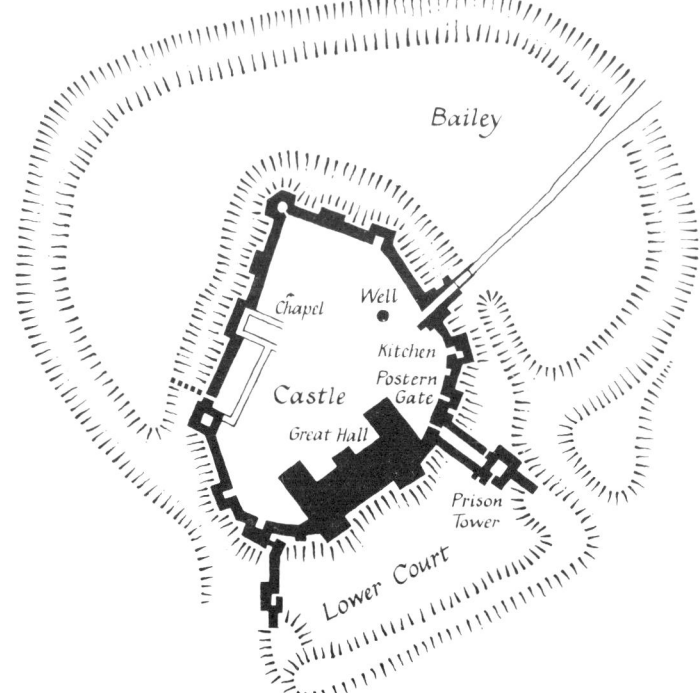

Framlingham Castle, Suffolk. What is the main difference between this and Dover Castle?

Plan of Framlingham Castle

Bailey

Chapel

Well

Kitchen

Castle

Postern Gate

Great Hall

Prison Tower

Lower Court

This thinking led to two develop-
ments. The first was that castles
began to be built without a keep.
A great circular wall was thrown up
and along its length towers were
erected. As we know, these towers
were built so that they overlooked the
walls. Each tower was connected
to the next through a corridor
built into the wall itself and there
were only a few entrances to the
towers and walk-ways at ground
level. Each tower could also be shut
off from the next. This meant that
even if part of the wall were destroyed
and the courtyard reached, each
tower could continue to defend itself. Every tower was therefore a
a small keep. Castles of this type are
known as castles of **enceinte.** Along
the inside of the wall in the courtyard, were the lord's hall, the chapel,
stables, storehouses and accommoda-
tion for all the servants and soldiers
who lived within. A famous castle of
this type is at Framlingham in
Suffolk.

As we have seen, the gatehouse of a
castle of this type was particularly
important and all sorts of defensive
mechanisms were built into it (see
Chapter 4).

But we must not think that this was
the end of the development of the
castle. Let's go back for a moment to
where we began – with the motte and
bailey castle. In this early castle the
strongest part was the motte. It was
the final place of refuge – the place

the lord retreated to when all the
rest of the castle had been overcome.
It was away from the centre of the
battle – it was really only a safe place
in which to hide! But by the time of
Edward I, the strongest place of all
within the walls of the 'new' castles
was the gatehouse – with portcullis,
drawbridge, folding doors and
murder holes.

It should come as no surprise to
learn that castles of this type are
known as **keep gatehouses.** The
safe place has been brought forward
from the centre of the castle to the
very front. Here – at the very centre
of the likely attack – the castellan or
constable (captain of the castle)
could direct the defence. The constable could also defend the gatehouse when the rest of the castle had
been overrun. This was important in
an age when soldiers sometimes
changed sides during a war for extra
money. The constable would put his
most trusted men in the gatehouse,
knowing that even if the rest of the
defenders deserted him he could re-
main in command of the strongest
part of the building.

The only trouble with this arrange-
ment was that sieges and battles were
not all that common – and the keep
was also supposed to be a place in
which to live. How would you like
to live in a house with all the gear for
lifting the portcullis in your front
room and the mechanism for moving
the drawbridge in your bedroom?

Some keep gatehouses were built on a
triangular plan like Caerlaverock Castle,
Dumfries

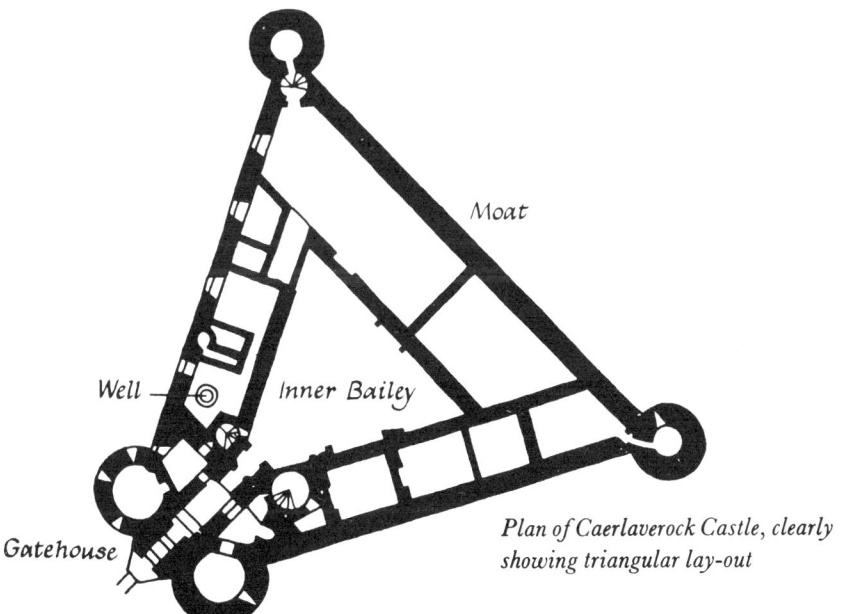

Moat

Well — Inner Bailey

Gatehouse

Plan of Caerlaverock Castle, clearly
showing triangular lay-out

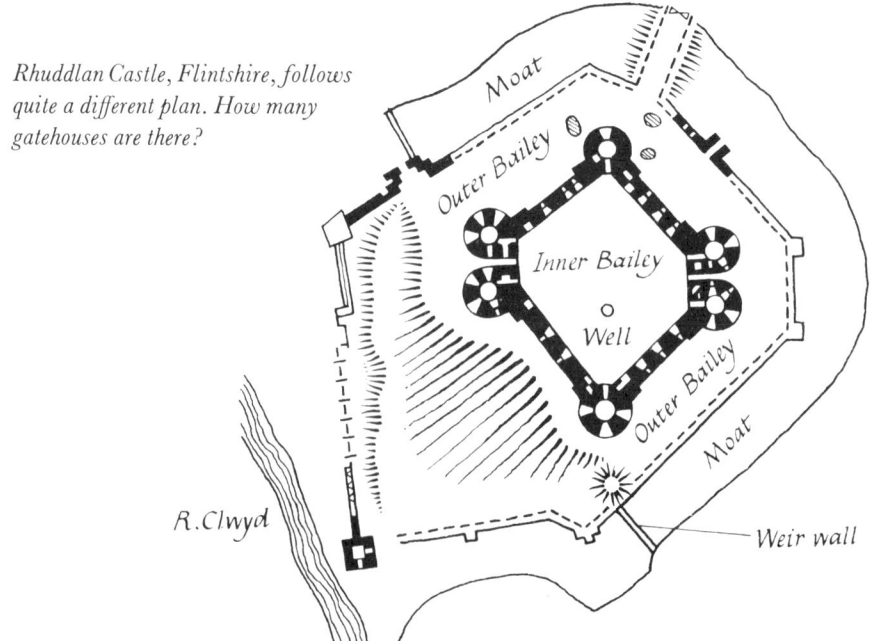

Here at Harlech Castle, Merionethshire,
the plan is based upon a square

Rhuddlan Castle, Flintshire, follows
quite a different plan. How many
gatehouses are there?

Moat

Outer Bailey

Inner Bailey

o
Well

Outer Bailey

Moat

R. Clwyd

Weir wall

The keep gatehouses fell out of favour because they just weren't comfortable to live in – and as the Middle Ages drew to a close, comfort mattered to those who lived in fortified houses and who paid for them to be built.

The development of the castle in the reign of Edward I (who built a whole string of castles across Wales, including Harlech and Rhuddlan) owed much to knowledge gained in the Crusades. One thing that military architects learned from the battles with the Turks was that castles could have defences at two levels. If the inner walls and towers were constructed so that they overlooked the outer walls, the enemy could be attacked from two different heights at the same time. Siege weapons would also be kept at a distance away from the gatehouse or 'heart' of the defence. Edward's architect – Master James of St George – built a perfect example of this type of castle at Beaumaris in Anglesey. There are two gatehouses and all of the inner towers could be

Beaumaris Castle curtain wall

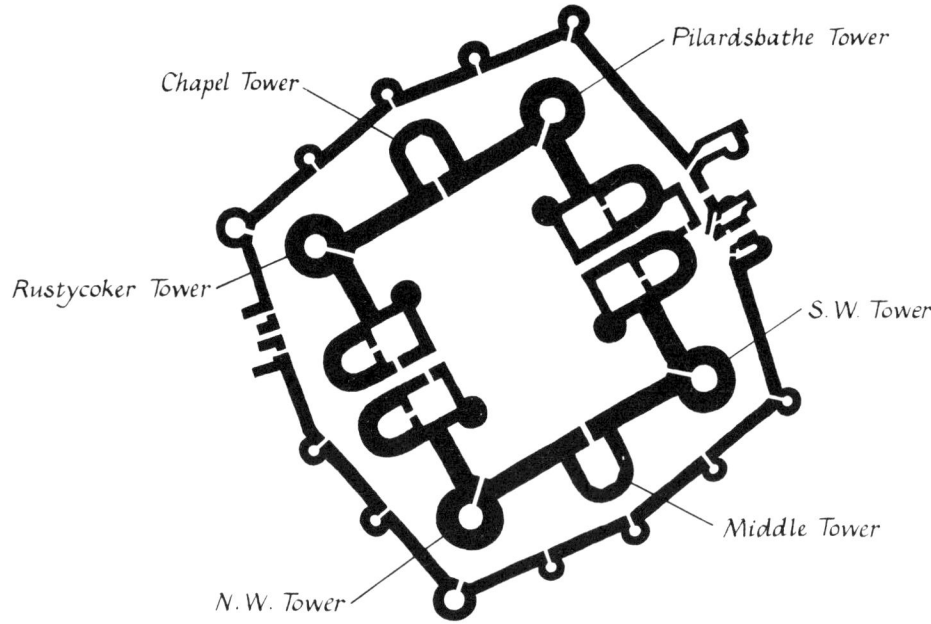

Plan of Beaumaris Castle. What is the
shape formed by the curtain walls?
Compare this plan with those of Orford,
Rochester, Framlingham, Caerlaverock,
Harlech and Rhuddlan

used to give covering fire over the heads of the defenders manning the outer walls. This is sometimes known as a **concentric castle.**

Even though gunpowder, first used at the battle of Crécy in 1346, was slowly beginning to change the style of warfare, castles continued to be built. But from 1380 onwards, they tended to be small and rectangular. They housed a lord and his paid re-tainers. The fortifications – round or square towers, a gatehouse and a moat – were still there, but the whole idea of the design was to provide a house in which the lord could live in comfort and safety and which would also allow defenders to move easily around the walls. You can see from the drawing of Bodiam Castle how the needs of comfortable living and defence were solved by building round a courtyard.

Here we can see the reason for the inner walls and towers being built to overlook the curtain wall and its supporting towers. The attackers have little hope of injuring the defenders on the inner walls and towers. All the ground in front of the castle is covered from above. There is no 'dead ground' that the defenders cannot overlook

Bodiam Castle, Sussex
Plan of Bodiam Castle – a square castle
built round courtyard (opposite)

Until this time (1400s) castles had
been built of stone and wood (though
here and there Roman tiles and
bricks had been fitted in). But the
final phase of castle building saw
one more change – bricks were used
instead of stone. The most famous
brick castles still standing are Hurstmonceux (Sussex) and Tattershall
(Lincolnshire). These later castles –
though similar in many ways to those
of earlier times – have one new
feature . . . gun ports (or holes) for
guns.

And the development of the gun
marks the end of the great days of
knight and castle.

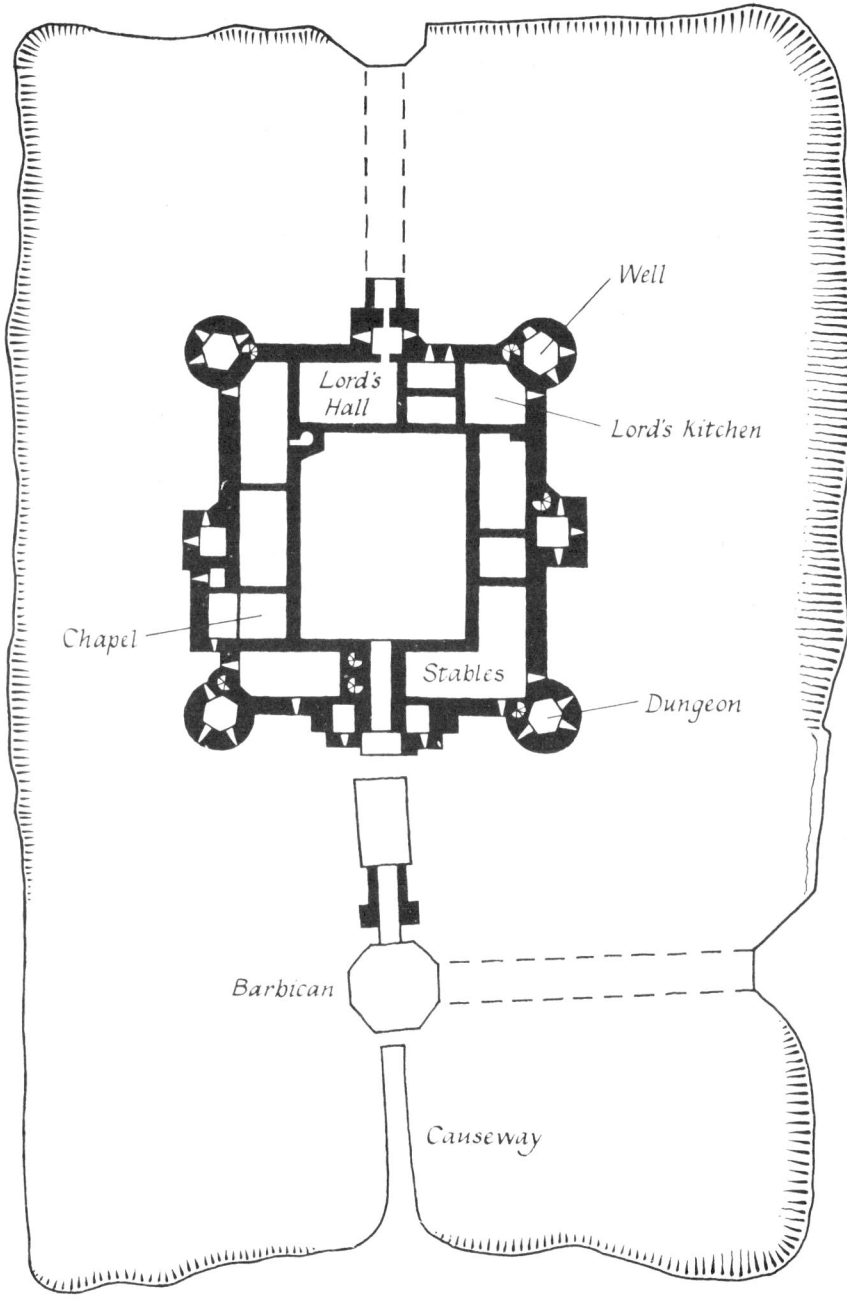

Tattershall Castle, Lincolnshire, built in brick between 1434 and 1446. How else does it differ from Rochester keep on page 20?

Strangely enough the last great series of castles to be built in England were commissioned by Henry VIII to house guns – guns to protect the coast of England from invasion from Europe. Henry's castles, at Deal and Walmer, were shaped rather like a flower. At the centre were the living quarters for the garrison and an ammunition store. Although these castles were simply gun-emplacements, the architect, a German called Von Haschenperg, also included a moat, a drawbridge and a gatehouse in his designs.

The age of castle building had come to an end. Nearly 500 years separate William the Conqueror and Henry VIII, and throughout this time the castle had been a feature of the English countryside. How many years separate us in time from Henry VIII?

The execution of Charles I during the Civil War (1649) also marks the death of the castle. Oliver Cromwell ordered that many castles should be 'slighted' – or so flattened by gunpowder that they could never be used in war again. Some castles escaped either because they supported Parliament throughout the Civil War or because they were not regarded as important. Some were slighted so thoroughly that little now remains but a pile of debris or a toppled tower. Others were only partially destroyed and, though roofless, enable us still to imagine them as once they were.

Hurstmonceux Castle, Sussex. A late castle built of brick

Camber Castle, Sussex, built by Henry VIII

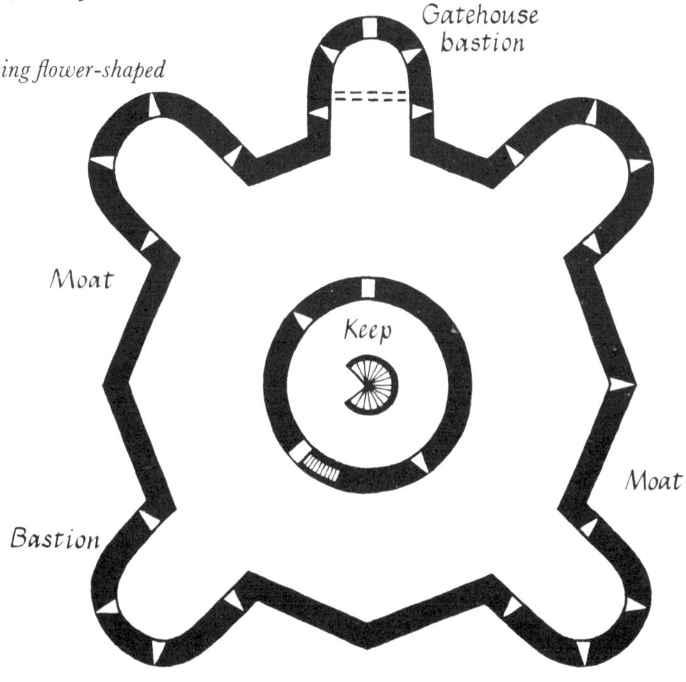

Plan of Camber showing flower-shaped lay-out

Gatehouse bastion

Moat

Keep

Moat

Bastion

The siege of Corfe Castle, Dorset. This castle was bravely defended by Lady Bankes for Charles I but was almost totally destroyed by the Parliamentarians . . .

*. . . and this is what it looks like today
from the village of Corfe*

3 Looking and recording

In the previous chapter we saw that a castle was both a military stronghold and a home for a great number of people. These two different functions meant that some parts of the castle were entirely military while other parts were purely domestic. Let me make this clearer by giving an example. Few castles were built without portcullis and chapel. The **portcullis** was a piece of military equipment – it was there for defence. The **chapel,** on the other hand, was a place for prayer and quiet; a place for priest and ladies rather than for knight and soldier. When visiting a castle it is often helpful to try to divide the buildings in this way. You might, for example, like to concentrate upon the military skills of the architect or to look entirely for evidence of ordinary everyday life within the walls.

A notebook or sketchpad (together with a range of felt-tipped pens, crayons and pencils) and a camera are very useful pieces of equipment to take on visits. Try to be selective in the things you record. You might, for example, look at only one aspect of castle architecture (like gatehouse defence) and make a scrapbook,

illustrating the styles of different periods. The study could be further limited by concentrating upon a particular area (like North Wales or the Scottish Borders) or upon a single county.

Or you might prefer your study to be more wide-ranging, taking note only of the more unusual aspects of the castles you visit. No one, for example, as far as I know, has written a book on 'carvings in castles' or 'castle fireplace decoration'. Your book may be the first! If you decided to make this your study how would you record your findings? Whether you use a camera or make a sketch in crayon, you must remember to note the date of your visit, the name of the castle you visited and the exact situation within the building of the object you photographed or drew. It will also be of interest to record the sort of materials used by the builder, for the type and quality of the materials used will have a marked effect upon the quality and style of workmanship.

Plans are another interesting thing to collect – they tell us a great deal about the development of a site. The

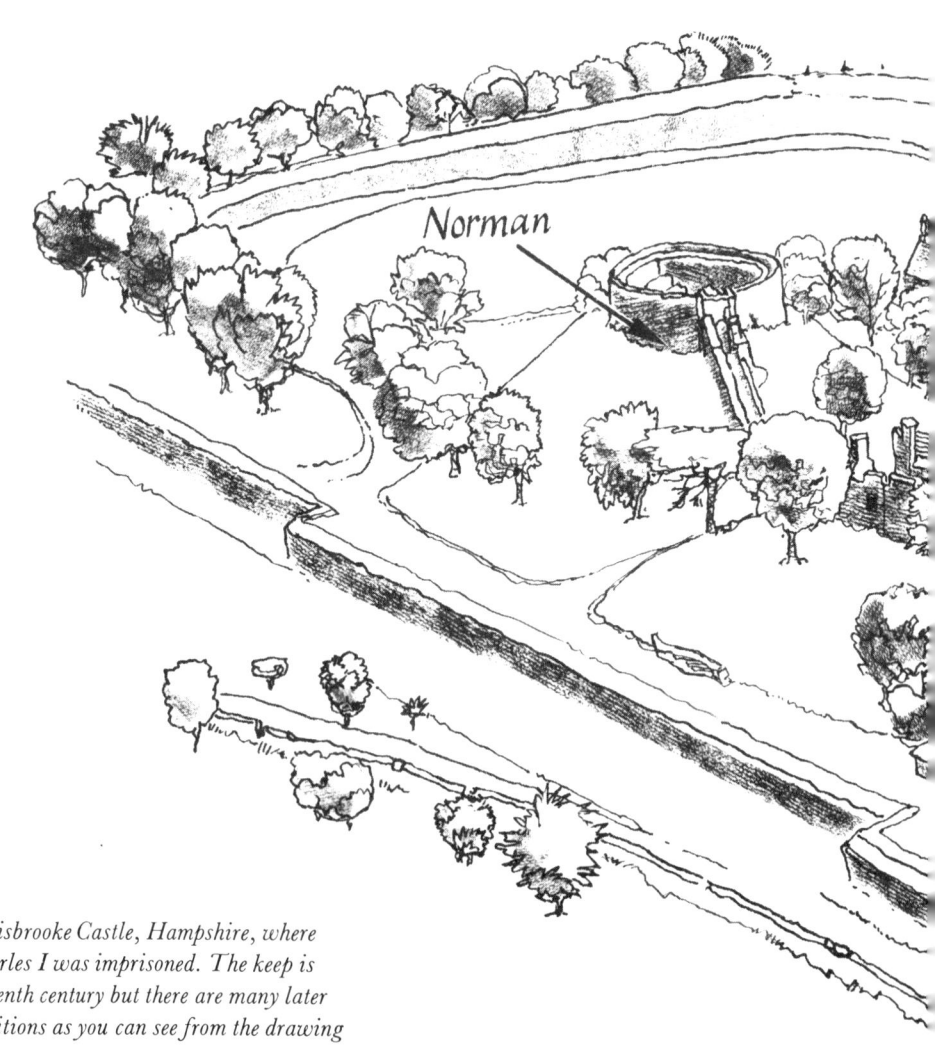

Norman

Carisbrooke Castle, Hampshire, where
Charles I was imprisoned. The keep is
eleventh century but there are many later
additions as you can see from the drawing

plans can either be drawn free-hand or copied from guide books. Plans show both the earthworks and the buildings and walls. By careful colouring, the gradual growth of the castle over the centuries can be clearly shown.

However, drawing and photography might not be your particular gift. Remember that a diary is an excellent method of keeping a record of things seen and experienced and that picture postcards may be used to illustrate the pages.

But whatever you decide to record, a simple survey chart completed during the visit will certainly help you recall all the important facts about a particular site.

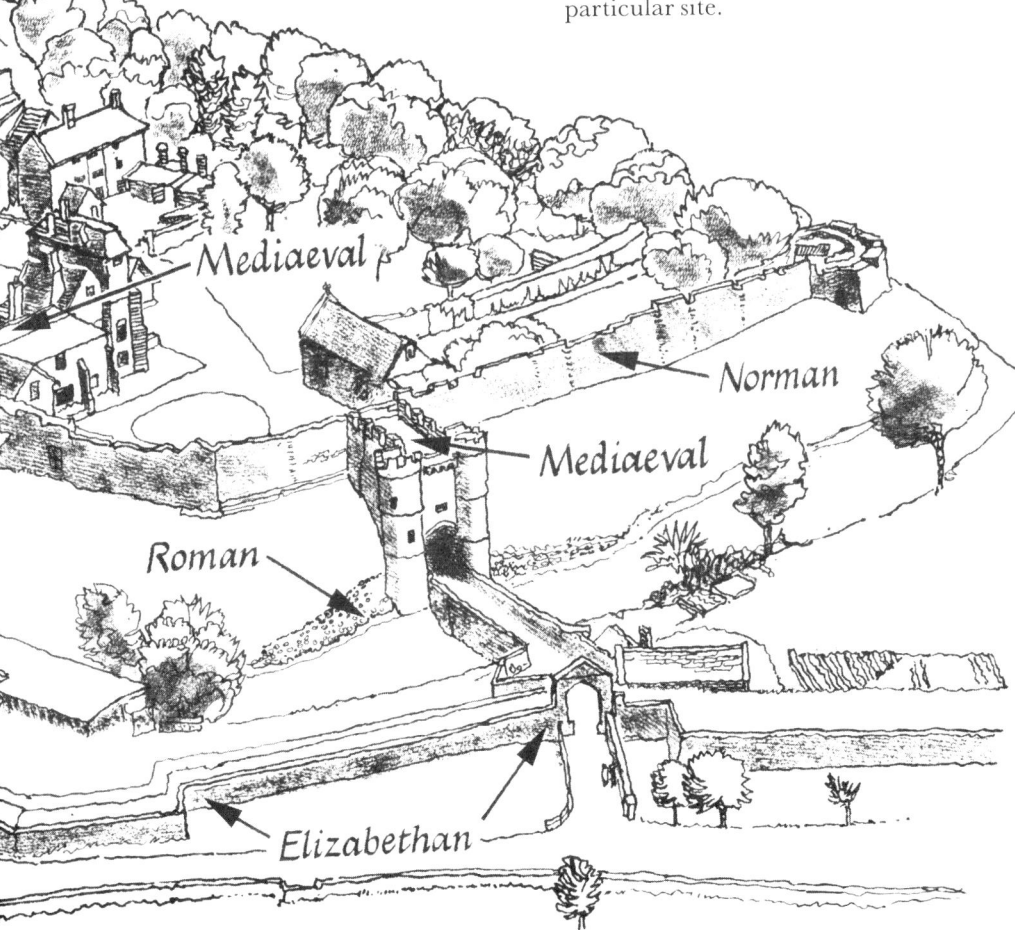

Castle Survey No. 12

Name of Castle Castle Rising (nr. Kings Lynn)

County Norfolk

Built by Earl of Sussex

Date of visit June 27th. 1972

Site dates from About 1150

Material used Dressed ashlar?

Norman window 2nd floor →

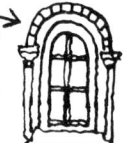

Castle plan

earth works and moat

keep

gate-house

Interesting features
military, domestic

Norman arch on first floor of keep - 5 arches all intertwined. Remains of Norman chapel in earth works.

Arcading

Famous associations

Was home of Isabella - mother of Edward III. Black Prince stayed here. Henry VIII gave it to Duke of Norfolk in 1544. Isabella's nickname was 'She wolf of France'

The door to the keep

Personal notes

An interesting Norman church in the village and some alms houses

Historical events

None that I discovered! But I have found out that Castle Rising used to be a harbour town, although it is now some way from the sea.

The Keep

4 Things to look for — military

In the first chapter, I explained how the castle developed and introduced some of the terms used to describe the geography of the castle (e.g. keep, motte, moat, gatehouse). Here we are not so much concerned with the pattern within the castle walls but the military aspects of the building. The questions can be applied to almost any castle and your answers will help build up a detailed survey of the castle you are visiting.

The approaches

1 Is there a moat?
Is it dry or water-filled?
Is there a curtain wall? Has the curtain wall mural towers? Are the mural towers rounded or square?

North platform and bastion towers, Caerphilly Castle, Glamorganshire. The oubliettes or pits in the wall behind each tower were once covered by pivoted trap-doors operated by a garrison in retreat

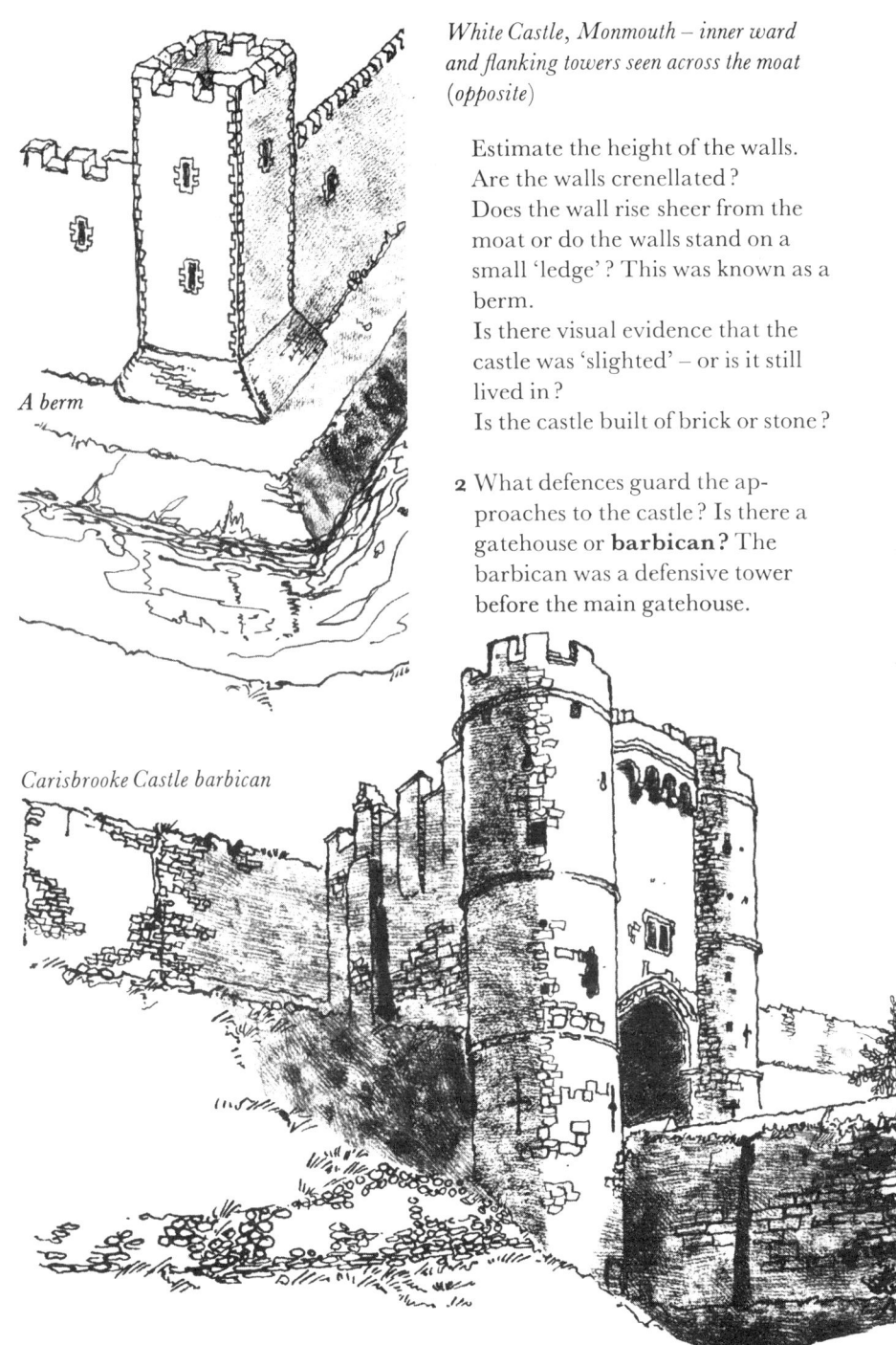

A berm

Carisbrooke Castle barbican

White Castle, Monmouth – inner ward and flanking towers seen across the moat (opposite)

Estimate the height of the walls. Are the walls crenellated?
Does the wall rise sheer from the moat or do the walls stand on a small 'ledge'? This was known as a berm.
Is there visual evidence that the castle was 'slighted' – or is it still lived in?
Is the castle built of brick or stone?

2 What defences guard the approaches to the castle? Is there a gatehouse or **barbican**? The barbican was a defensive tower before the main gatehouse.

3 Look at the base of the towers along
the curtain wall. Do they rise sheer
from the ground or do they thicken
and splay out at the base? Many
towers have an angled base to make
the wall more difficult to mine (it
was thicker) and so that missiles,
when dropped by defenders from
the walls above, would bounce out
upon the attackers. This con-
struction is known as a **batter**.

4 Examine the gatehouse.
Is there evidence that it housed a
drawbridge or a portcullis (many
gatehouses had both)?

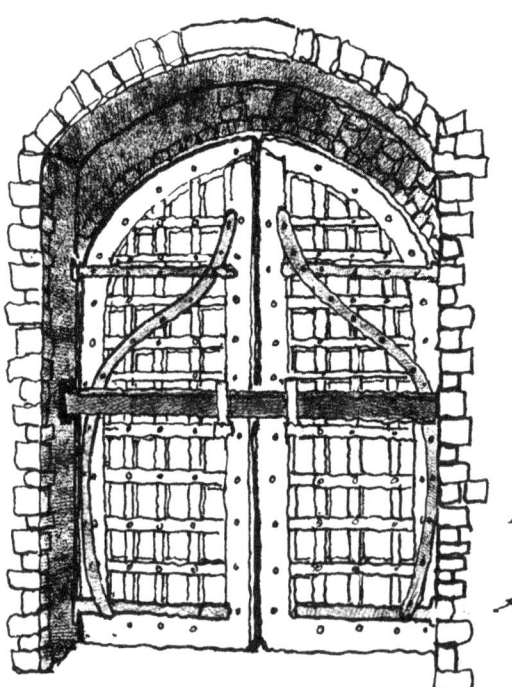

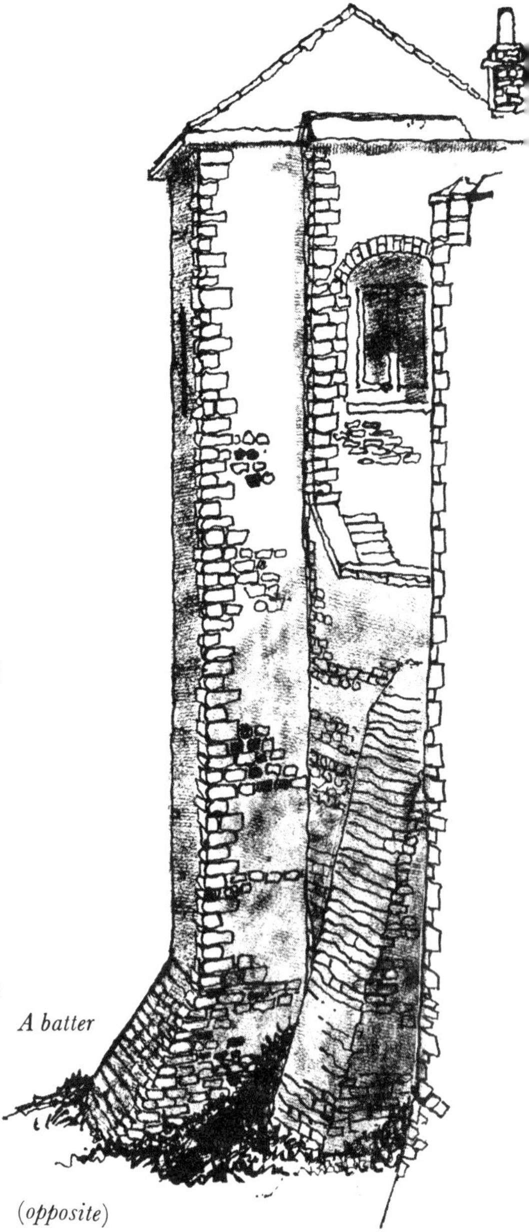

A batter

*Gatehouse door with wooden bolt in
position*

(*opposite*)
*Iron-studded oak doors from the upper
bailey to the barbican at Chepstow*

Are the grooves of the portcullis still visible?
Is there a deep channel in the wall on both sides of the entrance passageway which might have taken a wooden door bolt?
Are there any **murder holes** in the ceiling or arrow slits controlling the entrance?
Is the mechanism for raising the drawbridge or portcullis still visible? Is there evidence of a **counterpoise pit?** This was a common form of drawbridge and in many castle entrances, the pits can still be seen, even if the towers that once housed the bridge have fallen

Raised portcullis and murder holes for attack from above in Caldicot Castle gatehouse, Monmouthshire

Caerphilly Castle, Glamorganshire, with the raised portcullis as seen from the inside

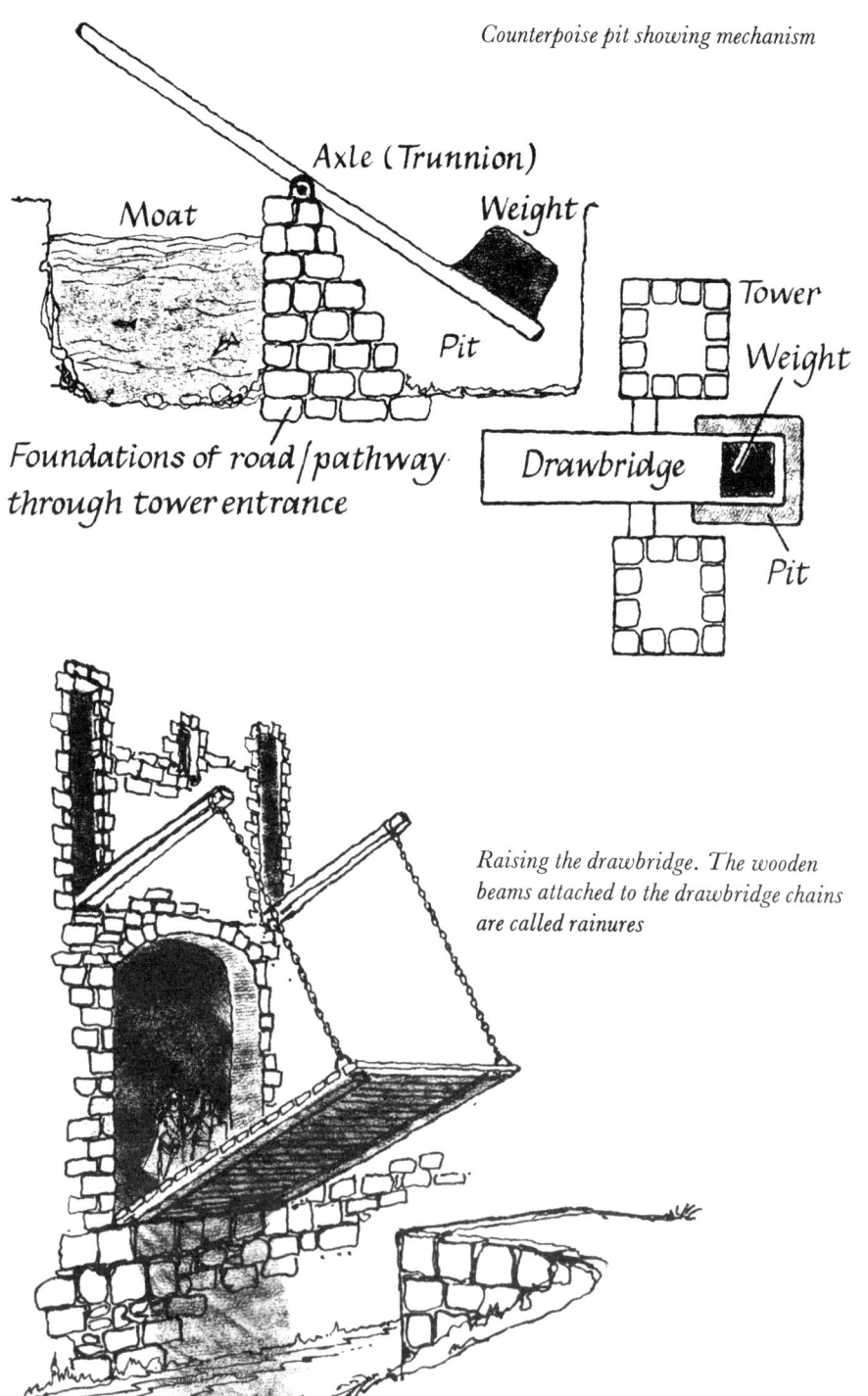

Counterpoise pit showing mechanism

Axle (Trunnion)

Moat

Weight

Pit

Tower

Weight

Drawbridge

Pit

Foundations of road/pathway
through tower entrance

*Raising the drawbridge. The wooden
beams attached to the drawbridge chains
are called rainures*

Raised drawbridge at Shirburn Castle,
Oxfordshire

into ruin (Denbigh has several
examples). The drawbridge was
sometimes raised by counterpoise
weights which were housed within
the tower.

Arrow slit in Marten's Tower, Chepstow

The Great Tower at Raglan, Monmouthshire has arrow slits cleverly converted to gunports at the base

5 Examine the **loop-holes** or **arrow slits** from the outside. What shape are they?

6 Are there any gunports?

7 Look at the plan of the castle. (There is usually a large framed one near the entrance or in the guide book.) Which other gates are marked? Look for the following:

Tower of London water gate

External steps leading to the wall walk at Beaumaris Castle, Anglesey

a) A postern gate (a side gate)
b) A sally port (a small side gate for defenders to slip out un-noticed)
c) A water gate

On the walls

1 Can you walk along the walls? How did you reach the wall walk – through an internal passageway or by external steps?

2 How thick are the walls? Are they as thick at the top as at their base? The pathway along the top of the walls is called an **allure** walk.

Internal steps to wall walk at Pickering
Castle, Yorkshire

Battlements of Marten's Tower,
Chepstow. Each merlon is pierced by an
arrow slit and surmounted by an
ornamental figure

Parapet and allure walk on the middle
bailey south wall, Chepstow

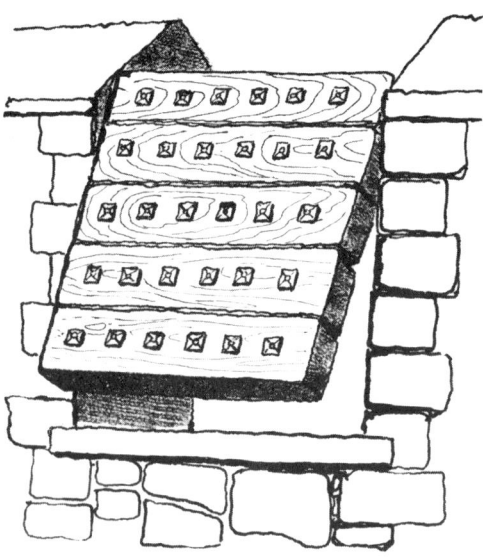

Added protection was given by wooden shutters fixed in the embrasures

A crossbow about to be fired from a wooden hoarding specially built so that attackers could be easily seen from above

3 Look at the crenellations. The solid sections are called **merlons** and the gaps are called **embrasures.** Sometimes we call these the **battlements.** Imagine that you are firing a crossbow from the walls through the embrasure. To give you further protection, a wooden shutter was often fixed between the merlons.

4 Are there any **putlog holes** at the base of the allure walk? These are holes in the wall below the crenellations. They were used to support a wooden hoarding which projected over the wall and on which defenders could climb to drop missiles directly upon their attackers.

Round keep on motte, Caldicot Castle, Monmouthshire. Notice the putlog holes at the top (opposite)

5 Examine the loop-holes or arrow slits from the inside. What do you notice about the shape? In the arrow slits built into the wall, space had to be left for the crossbow archer's assistant, who would wind up one bow whilst the archer was firing another.

6 Are any parts of the building **machicolated?** Machicolations are holes which jut out from the stone floor of the wall walks or parapets to give defenders the opportunity to drop missiles on their enemies below.

7 Are there any small turrets jutting out from near the top of a tower or

This is the same arrow slit as on page 56 (far left) but seen from the inside

A crossbow – chiefly used during the twelfth and thirteenth centuries. The bowstring was pulled back by a lever worked by the two handles at the end, the bolt (or arrow) was laid in the groove at the top and the string released by a trigger

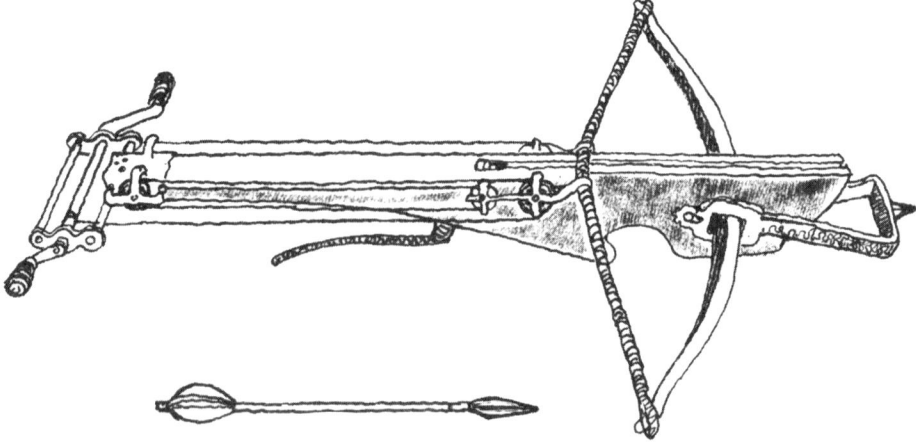

Twin half-hexagonal machicolated towers of Raglan Castle gatehouse (1450–69)

Conway Castle bartizans

Conway town walls

from the battlements? These
towers were constructed to enable
arrows to be fired at the enemy
from several different angles at the
same time (i.e. from archers on the
walls and from archers in the
turret). A small turret of this type
is called a **bartizan.**

*Plan of Denbigh Castle town walls. The
space between the town wall and the
mantlet was called the 'lists'. It might have
housed a tilt yard*

8 Do the walls of the castle adjoin the
town walls? Is there evidence of an
outer defensive wall beyond the
curtain wall? This wall was known
as the **mantlet.** A mantlet wall
had no towers along its length.

9 You will learn a great deal about
castle defences by continually
referring to the plans of the buildings you visit. Below is part of Denbigh Castle. Notice how the
mantlet wall gives greater protection to the town wall as well as
to the castle. Do you remember
what a sallyport was for?

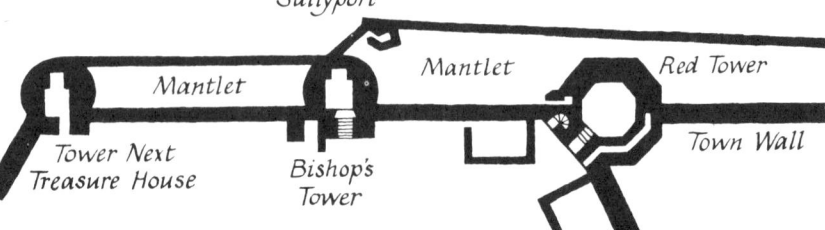

Sallyport
Mantlet — Mantlet — Red Tower
Tower Next Treasure House — Bishop's Tower — Town Wall

Forebuilding on Dover Castle keep

Staircase and entrances

1 What shape are the doorways to the defences? Are they wide or narrow?

2 Is there a keep? If there is, look for a forebuilding. The forebuilding was a defended entrance making the keep of the castle more difficult to storm. Does the forebuilding take the stairway to the first or second floor?

3 Is there a stairway leading into the upper stories of the keep? Is the staircase built around a central pillar? Which way does the staircase turn?
Imagine you are attacking the castle and have gained entrance to this stairway. In your hand you hold a sword. Could you use it easily? The defender on the stairway above you is right-handed. How would the staircase help him?

Dungeons and prison cells

Are there any parts of the castle which were used for holding prisoners? The basement of the keep was more likely to be used as a storehouse than as a dungeon. Sometimes an inscription carved by a prisoner may be seen. There are some famous examples in the Tower of London, Warwick and Norwich Castles.

Hand-to-hand combat on newel staircase

Prison wall graffitti in St Briavels Castle,
Gloucestershire. It reads, 'Wilam Bound
was takn the 11 off June 1677'

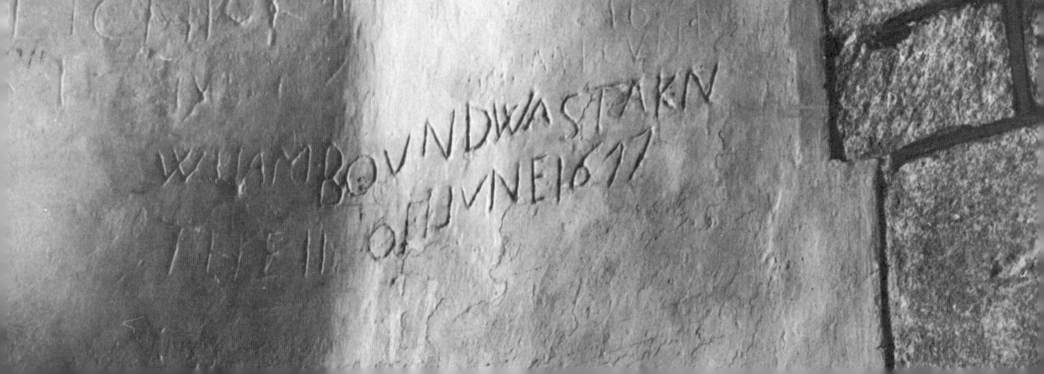

5 Things to look for—domestic

The castle was a place in which people lived. Indeed some castles are still being lived in today. Therefore, when we wander round a castle we should expect to find ordinary every-day things as well as things military. The questions which follow indicate some of the clues which, if studied carefully, tell us a great deal about domestic life long ago.

Food

1 Is there a kitchen? Historians suggest that much of the cooking would have been done out of doors. However, some later castles have quite impressive kitchens (e.g. Berkeley). Are there any ovens? At Ashby de la Zouch there is even a recess for hanging a cauldron.

Kitchen range in Kitchen Tower of Raglan Castle, Monmouthshire. There are floor-level gunports which pierce the back of the range

A dog-turned spit. A spit was a thin, pointed rod or bar on which meat was impaled so that it could be roasted in front of a fire. They were sometimes turned by hand, or by a dog who was placed in the wheel. His movements caused the spit to turn slowly in front of the fire

Orford Castle sink (right)

The well in the courtyard of Goodrich Castle, Herefordshire (below)

2 Is there a buttery marked on the plan? A buttery was where wine and ale was stored. Is it near the kitchen?

3 Is there a sink? At Orford Castle there is a sink let into the thickness of the wall and the drain runs through the wall to a spout outside.

4 Is there a basement or undercroft in which stores could be kept?

5 Where is the well situated? Is there more than one? Is it still filled with water today? How deep is it? The well at Dover is over 350 feet deep.

Living quarters

1 Is there a Lord's hall? This might be in the keep or be an elaborate building on its own. If the castle is ruinous look for holes in the internal walls for the floor joists (parallel beams supporting floor). The positioning of these holes will give you some idea of the size of the main rooms.

2 Is there a **solar** shown on the plan? This was the room in which the Lord of the castle slept with his family. It is usually found beyond the great hall.

3 Is there an **aumbry** (sometimes written ambry or almery)? This is a recess in the wall – a cupboard or safe for storing valuables. The aumbry probably had wooden doors. Look for the grooves in the stonework where the hinges were once fixed.

4 Are there any mural galleries running round the keep? Are there any small chambers or rooms off these galleries?

5 Are there any **garde robes?** This is a toilet (sometimes called a privy). They are usually found in a small chamber adjoining a mural gallery and overlook an external wall. A garde robe is simply a flat slab in which a circular hole has been cut. The waste fell into a cesspit or into the moat.
Look for the openings of the garde robes on the outside walls. They are often grouped in twos or threes so that the waste could be more easily channelled.

6 Are there any crests which record ownership of the castle? Compare the crests with any in the nearby village or town (on the public house sign, for example, and on tombs in the church).

7 Are there any interesting carvings on corbels, gargoyles or woodwork? A **corbel** is a stone jutting from a wall to support a beam or pillar. A **gargoyle** is a water spout which threw water from the upper levels of the building.

(Overleaf)
Romanesque arcade in the Great Tower, Chepstow. The two round windows were added later, probably for ventilation

(*On previous page*)
The Great Hall in Stokesay Castle,
Shropshire

Mural galleries – this one is Norman . . .   . . . and this one Gothic

Great Hall hung with shields and banners, Caerphilly Castle, Glamorganshire

Canopy over state bedroom window in Raglan Castle, Monmouthshire. The heraldic motifs are those of the Herbert family and show bascules or drawbridge counterpoises alternating with large *fluted shields which were probably painted*

The arms of Newcastle-upon-Tyne
depicting three machicolated castles with
bartizans

Harwich has a representation of a portcullis

Castles have always been a favourite symbol. At the top is a 1457 silverware mark for Edinburgh. Many coins, medallions and regimental badges also have castles on them: on the left is Rochester Castle and on the right Exeter Castle on the badge of the Devonshire and Dorset Regiment

Also look for castles on inn signs, and for contemporary drawings of them in old books and guides

A tomb in Skenfrith Church, Monmouth-shire, with the arms of the Cecils, the family of Ann, wife of John ap Philip Morgan who was the last governor of the 'Three Castles' – Grosmont, Skenfrith and White Castle

Serpent carving on the corner of Stokesay Castle gatehouse (left)

(Above right)
Gargoyle on the gatehouse tower of Raglan Castle, Monmouthshire. What are the holes around the top called?

(Below right)
Machicolations supported by sculpted corbels on Caldicot Castle gatehouse. Notice also the quatrefoil window

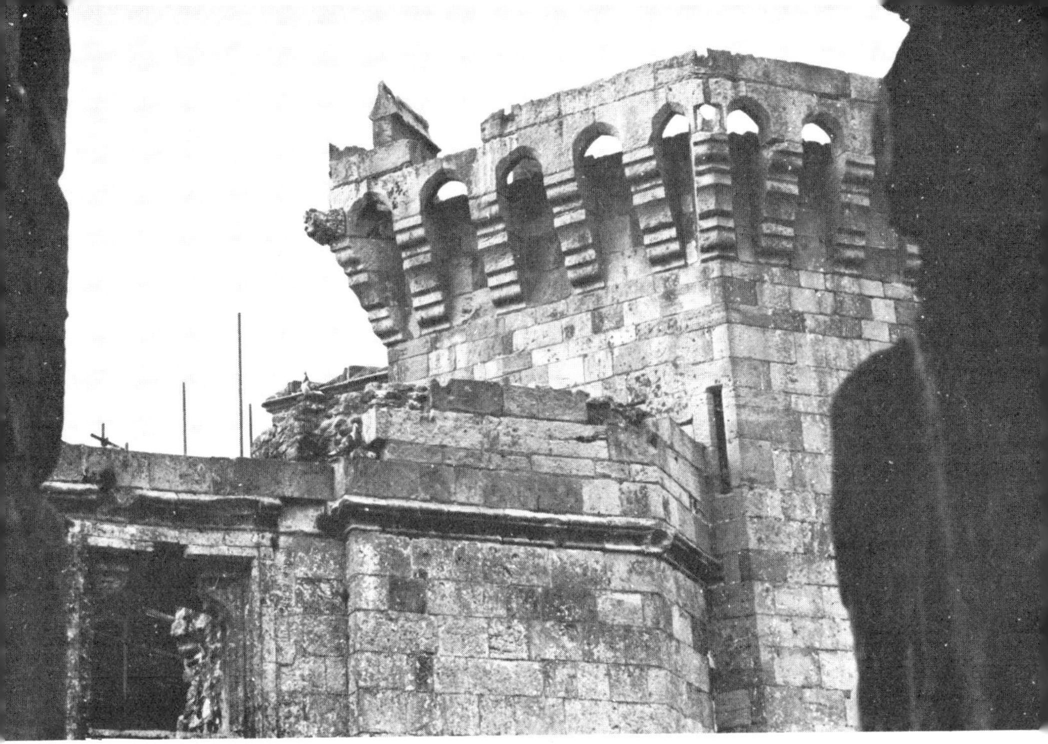

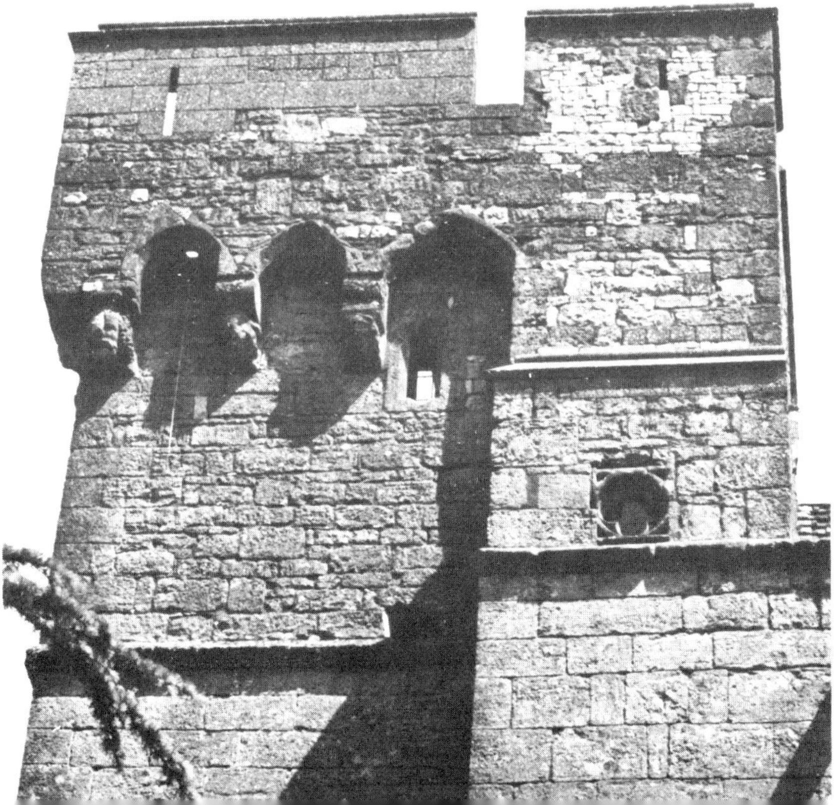

*Line of corbels inside west wall of
Chepstow Castle barbican*

*Floriated carving round east window of
chapel in Marten's Tower, Chepstow
(right)*

Lighting and heating

1 What shape are the windows? How
did the early castle builders make
sure that as much light as possible
came through the narrow slit?
The windows on the left and right
are different. Yet both styles may
be seen at the same castle
(Chepstow). How many different
window styles can you find in one
castle?

(left)
*Another kind of window from Chepstow
Castle. What else can you see?*

*Two-sixteenth-century fireplaces on the
west side of Chepstow's lower bailey*

*Chimney pot on Grosmont Castle,
Monmouthshire*

2 How many fireplaces can you find?
Some will be seen in quite un-
expected places – in guard rooms
in the towers at the corners of the
keep.
In the early castles a great open
fire in the Lord's hall provided
most of the heat. The smoke went
out through an opening in the
ceiling. This was somewhat dirty –
and fireplaces were introduced.
Fireplaces need chimney breasts.

Are there any chimney pots in the
towers along the curtain wall?

Religion

1 Is there a **chapel**?
This might be built within the
keep or gatehouse or it might be in
a separate building.

*Caerphilly Castle chapel, with a piscina
and a sedilia. Do you know what these
were for? 'On Location : Churches'
might help*

2 Is there more than one chapel?

3 Are there any priests' rooms
   nearby?

*The sole remains of the chapel in Raglan
Castle – vaulting ribs and corbel heads*

*The Round Chapel, Ludlow Castle,
Shropshire. This is one of only five round
Norman chapels in Britain*

6 Some questions to ask

When you have really looked at the castle you are visiting, try to find answers to some of the questions below. You might find that the castle guide book will be of help. The custodian (or the museum curator) will probably be able to give you the 'odd' information you can't find in books – stories of brave knights and bad barons and legends of saints (like St Margaret) and ghosts who return to haunt the rooms they once lived in.

1 When was the castle last lived in?

2 Who owned it throughout the greater part of its history?

3 Who owns it now?

4 What do we know about the builder?

5 Why do you think the castle was built – to guard a port, protect a town, to control a road or river crossing?

6 Did the castle house any famous people or play a part in any famous historical event?

7 Is the castle one of a number commissioned by the same king? Are the others similar to it? (An interesting exercise this if you visit all the Edwardian castles of North Wales.)

8 Are there any prints to show the castle as it once was? Look for these in local bookshops, the local museum and in guide books.

9 Is there a museum in the castle? What relics were of particular interest?

10 Have military terms been incorporated in the names of streets around the castle? (e.g. Castle Hill, Inner Ward, The Bailey).

11 Are people who were associated with the castle buried or commemorated in the local church?

*A postern gate (Woodstock Tower of
Caldicot Castle, Monmouthshire) with a
sculpted quatrefoil stone on the lower door
jamb with the name of 'Thomas' on it –
the castle's fourteenth-century builder,
Thomas Woodstock*

A castle maintained by the Department of
the Environment who ensure the public's
safety and provide easy access. This is the
centrally placed thirteenth-century round
keep of Skenfrith Castle in Monmouthshire

A castle still privately owned and unfortunately in a dangerous and overgrown state – Pen-coed Castle, also in Monmouthshire

The stone-carved hunting horn on a chimney of St Briavel's Castle, Gloucestershire, gives an indication of its earlier use as a royal hunting lodge. It is now a Youth Hostel

*Chepstow Castle from the north, guarding
the River Wye*

7 Imaginings

As castle defence improved, the machines that the attackers used became more and more complicated. Imagine that you are involved in a battle around the castle walls. Here are some of the weapons you might see.

Mining

Sappers went forward and, protected by a wooden screen, dug a pit beneath the foundations of a wall (usually at a corner, its weakest part). They propped the wall above the hole with wooden struts. The hole was then filled with dry timber and animal fat and fired. The fire burned the supporting struts and the wall, now unsupported, fell to the ground.

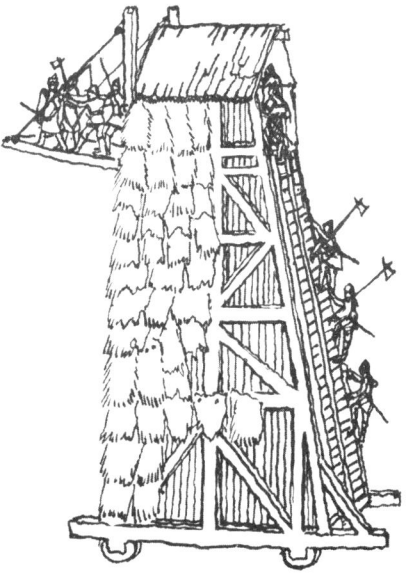

A siege tower was wheeled up to the walls to enable the attackers to storm the castle

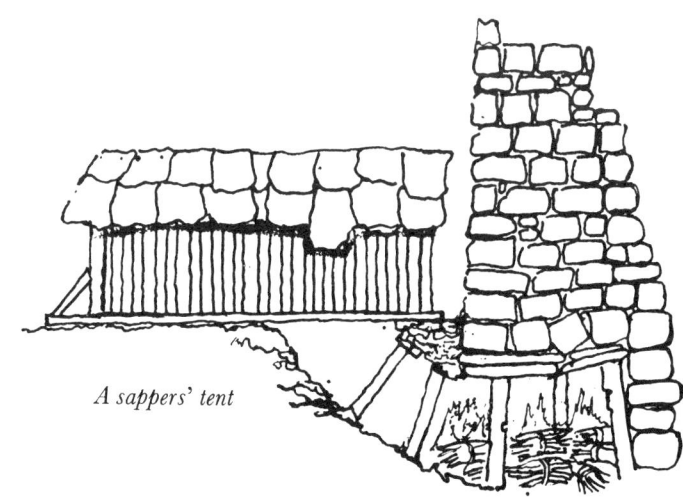

A sappers' tent

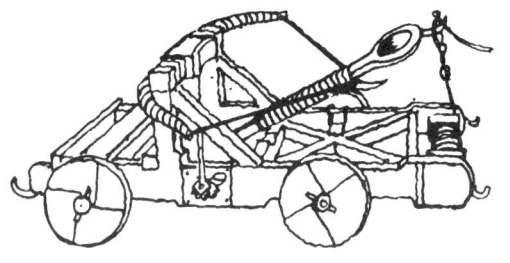

A mangonel was rather like a big
catapult for casting huge boulders
against the walls

A protective shield on wheels was called a
mantlet

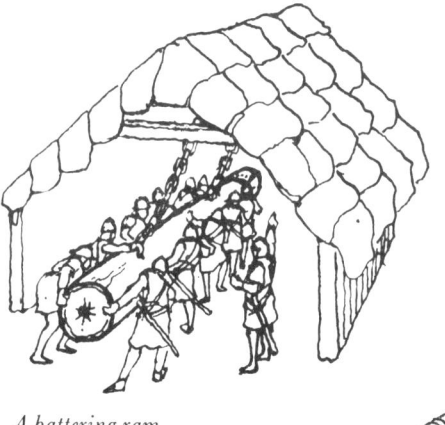

A battering ram

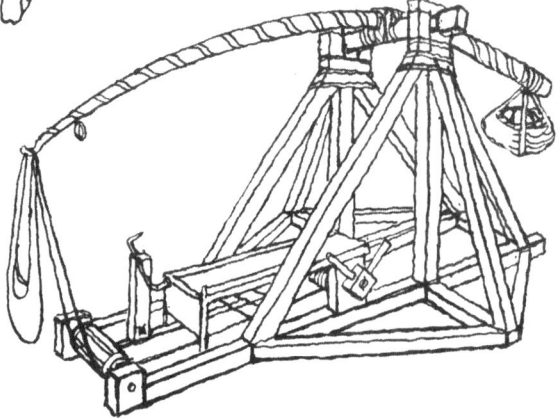

Another kind of catapult for casting
stones against the defences. This was
called a trebuchet

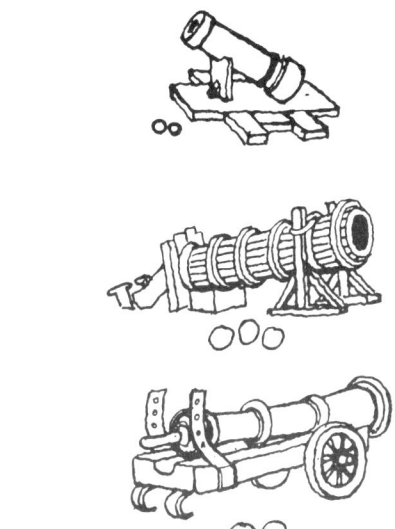

This weapon, called a ballista, was used to hurl stones as well as arrows against the castle. Our word 'ballistic' comes from the Greek word 'ballo' meaning to throw

Some early cannon

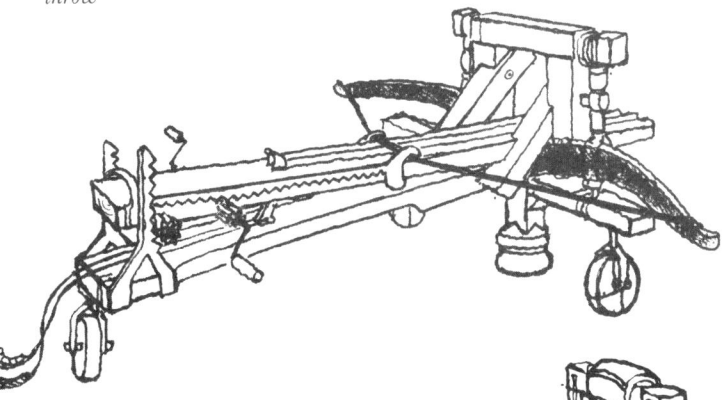

This is an arblast – a crossbow on wheels

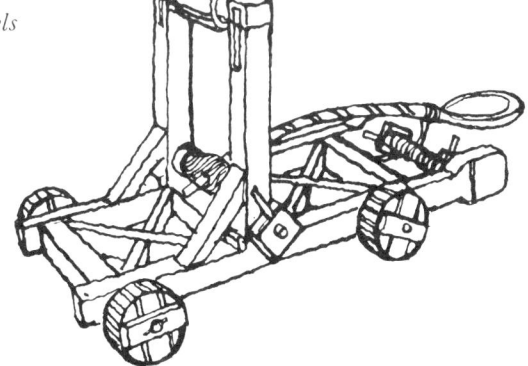

A mangon – another ballistics weapon

8 Dating the building

Guide books often refer to the reign of a particular king, but omit to give the date. This chart might help you.

RULER	CAME TO THRONE	BUILDING STYLE
*Edward the Confessor	1042	Norman (though not general until
Harold Godwinson	1066	after 1066)
William I	1066	
William II	1087	
Henry I	1100	
Stephen/Matilda	1035	
Henry II	1154	
Richard I	1189	
John	1199	Early English 'Gothic'
Henry III	1216	
Edward I	1272	leading onto
Edward II	1307	
Edward III	1327	Decorated
Richard II	1377	Perpendicular
Henry IV	1399	
Henry V	1413	
Henry VI	1422	
Edward IV	1461	
Edward V	1483	
Richard III	1483	
Henry VII	1485	
Henry VIII	1509	
Edward VI	1547	Renaissance
Mary	1553	
Elizabeth I	1558	
James I	1603	
Charles I	1625	

* Edward spent much of his childhood in Normandy and had many Norman courtiers.

Commonwealth	1649	
(Oliver Cromwell		
Richard Cromwell)		
Charles II	1660	
James II	1685	
William & Mary	1689	
Anne	1702	Georgian
George I	1714	
George II	1727	
George III	1760	
George IV	1820	
William IV	1830	
Victoria	1837	Gothic revival
Edward VII	1901	
George V	1910	
Edward VIII	1936	Contemporary
George VI	1936	
Elizabeth II	1952	

9 A summary of architectural terms

Allure	A wall walk along a curtain wall.
Ashlar	Dressed and cut stone.
Aumbry	A recess in a wall (usually a cupboard).
Bailey	The courtyard.
Barbican	Gateway.
Bartizan	Small turret built into face of curtain wall or tower.
Bastion	Corner fortification.
Batter	Angled base to foot of tower or wall.
Berm	Earth or stone ledge between moat and curtain wall.
Buttery	Wine and ale store.
Castellan	Captain of a castle.
Corbel	Stone bracket for supporting a projecting battlement or pillar.
Crenellations	Battlements on top of wall.
Curtain	The wall enclosing the courtyard of a castle.
Donjon	The keep.
Embrasure	Open space in a crenellation through which the archer shoots.
Forebuilding	Outbuilding protecting entrance to keep.
Garde robe	A toilet.
Gargoyle	A water spout.
Gatehouse	Castle entrance.
Keep	The donjon or safe place – the centre of the defences.
Loop-hole	A slit in a wall for ventilation or for shooting through.
Louver	An opening (often to let smoke escape from a central fire).
Machicolation	Spaces (holes) left between corbels to enable defenders to throw missiles downwards upon the attackers.
Mantlet	Defensive wall beyond the curtain wall.
Merlons	Solid portions of a crenellation.

Meurtrière	A murder hole, usually found in an entrance passage (e.g. in the gatehouse).
Moat	Ditch, often water-filled, which ran round castle.
Motte	Earthen mound of an early castle.
Newel	Staircase built round central pillar.
Portcullis	An iron or wood grating which could be dropped to block an entrance or passage.
Postern	Side gate.
Putlogs	Beams which supported a projecting timber gallery. Putlog holes are found just below the crenellations on the battlements.
Rainures	Beams for raising drawbridge.
Sally port	Side gate.
Shell (keep)	A circular stone wall enclosing donjon and courtyard.
Slight	Ruin a castle so that it can never again be used in time of siege.
Undercroft	Store place (usually a basement).
Ward	The courtyard enclosure of a castle.